A WOMAN'S WILDERNESS:

Navigating Life as a Woman and Mother

BY RGE KEY

Some content created with the use of Designrr.io. Information for the inspirational stories of the women were obtained from Wikipedia.

Contents

Introduction 1

Chapter 1.
Navigating Power Imbalance and Vulnerability 6

Chapter 2.
The Desert Within - The Weight of Isolation 9

Chapter 3.
Struggling in the Desert - The Strength of a Woman and Mother 14

Chapter 4.
Acknowledgement of the Marginalized - The Message of Comfort.. 17

Chapter 5.
Finding the Well of Water Within – Cultivating Inner Resources 23

Chapter 6.
Seeking Community - The Quest for Belonging.................. 35

Chapter 7.
Speaking into the Future 39

Chapter 8.
Reclaiming the Narrative - Write Your Own Story 46

Chapter 9.
The Permission to Love and Be Loved Again 50

Chapter 10.
Finding Rest and Peace..56

Chapter 11.
Inspirational Stories of Ten Women Who Rewrote Their Stories.. 61

Chapter 12.
Healing and Growth...70

Introduction

In countless homes around the world, mothers rise before dawn, carrying the weight of both provider and caregiver on their shoulders. They lace up shoes, pack lunches, and check homework, often wondering how they'll balance it all. Their days are a whirlwind of work, school pickups, and bedtime routines, all while managing the worries of finances, stability, and future dreams for their children. Despite the challenges, they find strength in their love and dedication, navigating a world that often overlooks their resilience and underestimates their worth.

This story is as old as time. Long ago, there was another mother facing the wilderness of single parenthood—a woman named Hagar. Once a servant in Abraham and Sarah's household, she had been thrust into motherhood with little choice or support. When circumstances changed, Hagar was left alone with her young son, Ishmael, to journey into the desert with nothing but her faith and her fierce determination to protect her child. Rejected and isolated, she wandered through the wilderness, unsure of what lay ahead. But in the harshest of landscapes, Hagar's story became one of survival, resilience, and the discovery of divine support.

Genesis 21:8-21

"Now the child grew and was weaned. And on the day Isaac was weaned, Abraham held a great feast. But Sarah saw the son whom Hagar the Egyptian had borne to Abraham mocking, 10 and she said to Abraham, "Get rid of that slave woman and her son, for that woman's son will never share in the inheritance with my son Isaac." 11 The matter distressed Abraham greatly because it concerned his son. 12 But God said to him, "Do not be so distressed about the boy and your slave woman. Listen to whatever Sarah tells you, because it is through Isaac that your offspring will be reckoned. 13 As for the son of the slave woman, I will make him into a great nation because he is your offspring."

14 So Abraham rose early in the morning and took bread and a skin of water and gave them to Hagar, putting them on her shoulder, along with the child, and sent her away. And she departed and wandered in the wilderness of Beersheba. 15 The water in the skin ran out, and she cast the child under one of the bushes. 16 Then she went and sat down opposite him a good way off, about a bowshot away, for she said, "Do not let me see the boy die." And as she sat opposite him, she wept aloud.

17 God heard the boy crying, and the angel of God called to Hagar from heaven and said to her, "What is the matter, Hagar? Do not be afraid; God has heard the boy crying as he lies there. 18 Lift the boy up and take him by the hand, for I will make him into a great nation." 19 Then God opened her eyes, and she saw a well of water. She went and filled the skin with water and gave the boy a drink. 20 God was with the boy as he grew up. He lived in the desert and became an archer. He lived in the wilderness of Paran, and his mother got a wife for him from Egypt."

Hagar, the Egyptian maidservant of Sarah, emerges as a powerful icon in the biblical narrative, particularly for mothers and women who feel marginalized. Her story is not just a tale of survival; it is a profound testament to resilience and strength in the face of adversity. Hagar's journey through the desert symbolizes the struggles many women experience today, especially those navigating the complexities of motherhood. She teaches us that even in the harshest of circumstances, one can find their voice, reclaim agency, and emerge as a beacon of hope for others.

In the face of abandonment and neglect, Hagar demonstrates remarkable courage. When Sarah, feeling threatened by Hagar's role as the mother of Abraham's child, mistreats her, Hagar flees into the wilderness. This act of fleeing is significant; it reflects the instinctive desire for self-preservation and dignity. For mothers, this resonates deeply as they often find themselves in challenging situations where they must prioritize their well-being and that of their children. Hagar's decision to escape her suffering is an empowering reminder that seeking a healthier environment is not only permissible but essential for growth and healing.

Hagar's encounter with the divine in the desert is a pivotal moment that underscores her significance as a feminist figure. God sees her in her plight and provides comfort and guidance, affirming her worth and purpose. This divine acknowledgment is crucial for marginalized women who often feel invisible in society. Hagar's experience reinforces the idea that every woman, regardless of her circumstances, deserves to be seen, heard, and valued. It also highlights the importance of spiritual growth, as it encourages women to seek their identity beyond societal labels and to embrace their inherent worth.

The lessons drawn from Hagar's narrative extend beyond individual resilience; they emphasize the necessity of community support. Hagar's story encourages women to connect with one another, share their experiences, and uplift each other. The bonds formed within a community can provide strength and encouragement, especially for mothers who may feel isolated. Hagar's story serves as a reminder that relationships can be navigated and redefined, and that finding a supportive network is vital to overcoming feelings of loneliness and despair.

Hagar represents the intersection of faith and feminism, showcasing how biblical narratives can empower contemporary women. Her story invites mothers to reflect on their journeys and to embrace their struggles as part of a larger narrative of resilience and strength. By reclaiming Hagar's voice, women today can find inspiration and hope, recognizing that their stories matter and that they, too, can carve out a space for themselves in a world that often marginalizes them. Through Hagar's journey, we learn that healing and empowerment are possible, and that even in isolation, we can find purpose and strength, both for ourselves and for those who follow in our footsteps.

Chapter One

Navigating Power Imbalance and Vulnerability

Many mothers, especially those whose partners are more powerful or influential, experience feelings of powerlessness. Their stories involve the real emotional and social challenges that come with navigating a situation where they may feel manipulated, coerced, or dismissed. In situations like these, women often bear the burden alone, facing stigma for being a mother while the man in question may escape scrutiny or responsibility. Hagar's story, however, suggests that God is aware of these complex, often unjust dynamics. The divine response in her life indicates that God not only sees but also deeply understands the challenges posed by such unequal relationships.

Hagar's relationship with Abraham is complicated by the vast differences in power between them. In this story, Hagar is a servant in the household of Abraham and Sarah. She is an Egyptian woman, marginalized by her status and her position in the family, yet her life is deeply impacted by the decisions of those in power around her. Sarah, who has been unable to conceive, offers Hagar to Abraham in an attempt to produce an heir. As Sarah's servant, Hagar had little say over her life or her body; she was instructed to bear a child for Abraham as part of an arrangement she did not initiate or necessarily want. This lack of agency resonates with many mothers today who find themselves in relationships marked by power imbalances, often with men who hold significant social, financial, or emotional influence over them. Such relationships can leave women vulnerable, sometimes in ways they cannot fully recognize until much later. Hagar becomes pregnant with Ishmael. This child brings her both a unique bond with Abraham's household and new vulnerabilities.

After Sarah later bears her own son, Isaac, tensions arise, and Hagar and Ishmael are cast out, left to face the harsh desert with limited resources. Hagar's story centers on this journey through the wilderness, where she reaches the brink of despair. Yet, it's in this moment of vulnerability that she has a transformative encounter with God, who provides for her needs, assures her of Ishmael's future, and gives her a sense of dignity and hope. This aspect of Hagar's story can bring comfort and solidarity to mothers who have faced similar dynamics. Her journey reassures them that their struggles are seen and that God values their lives and autonomy even if society and influential figures in their lives do not. God's awareness and response to Hagar's predicament underscore that their suffering matters, and their pain is not ignored in the divine story.

Chapter Two

The Desert Within - The Weight of Isolation

Hagar's story in the desert after being cast out from Abraham's household is a powerful narrative that speaks to the feelings of abandonment and isolation many mothers face today. When Sarah demands that Hagar and her son, Ishmael, be sent away, Hagar is left to navigate the wilderness with little more than survival essentials. This abandonment leaves her vulnerable, with no support system or community to lean on. The emotional toll of such an experience is significant, as it would be for any parent suddenly faced with the reality of providing alone for their child in an uncertain environment.

For modern mothers, especially those who were once part of a relationship or support system, Hagar's experience resonates as it mirrors the shock, fear, and isolation that can accompany unexpected single parenthood. This is especially true for those who are abandoned by partners who once promised support and companionship. Hagar's story validates the deep emotional journey of mothers who may find themselves feeling isolated from the rest of society or unsupported in their journey.

The weight of isolation can feel suffocating, especially for mothers navigating the complexities of life on their own. Just as Hagar found herself alone in the desert with her son Ishmael, many women today experience profound solitude, grappling with the challenges of raising children without the support of a partner. This isolation can be exacerbated by societal expectations, leading to feelings of inadequacy and despair. Hagar's journey illustrates the emotional turmoil that can arise from such circumstances, emphasizing the importance of recognizing and addressing these feelings.

In Hagar's story, isolation is not merely physical; it is deeply emotional and spiritual. As a modern woman, one might relate to Hagar's plight, feeling cast aside by a world that seems indifferent to her struggles. The desert symbolizes not only her physical surroundings but also the emotional landscape she traverses—marked by uncertainty, fear, and longing for connection. Each day can feel like a battle against the elements, where the heat represents societal pressures and the vast emptiness mirrors the loneliness many mothers face. Yet, within this narrative lies the potential for transformation and resilience.

The demands of motherhood, work, relationships, and personal well-being can leave us feeling overwhelmed, exhausted, and, at times, isolated. In the midst of these pressures, there is a subtle but dangerous lie that can creep into our hearts: "I am alone in this." This feeling of isolation can lead us to believe that we are the only ones experiencing our struggles, or that no one truly understands our pain.

But this belief is a lie that the enemy uses to keep us disconnected, discouraged, and ineffective. It's easy to fall into the trap of believing that no one else understands the weight we carry. Loneliness can feel overwhelming, and isolation becomes a natural response. We may retreat from friends, avoid reaching out for help, or feel like we should be able to handle everything on our own.

But the illusion of isolation is just that—a lie. It's based on the false belief that we are the only ones going through difficult times. The truth is, every woman and mother has moments of feeling overwhelmed and exhausted. We are not alone in our struggles. Others—whether in our immediate circle or across the world—are facing similar challenges.

The next time you feel the creeping thought that you are alone, recognize it for what it is: a lie. Remind yourself that God sees you, that He is with you, and that there are people around you who care and want to help. Speak truth to your heart—you are not alone in this, and you don't have to walk through life's struggles by yourself. It's clear from Scripture that isolation is not God's design for us. God has created us for community—first with Him, and then with each other. The antidote to the lie of isolation is connection.

Overcoming the weight of isolation requires a concerted effort to seek out community and support. Hagar's encounter with divine intervention in the wilderness serves as a powerful reminder that even in our darkest moments, hope can emerge. For mothers today, finding solace in shared experiences can be a lifeline. By connecting with others who understand their journey, women can begin to dismantle the walls of loneliness and foster a sense of belonging. Support groups, online communities, and friendships formed through shared challenges can provide the encouragement needed to navigate the complexities of motherhood.

Faith and doubt often coexist in the lives of mothers, particularly during times of crisis. Just as Hagar cried out in her despair, many women wrestle with their beliefs and question their purpose. This internal struggle can be isolating but also serves as a catalyst for growth. Embracing vulnerability allows for a deeper connection with oneself and with others, fostering an environment where healing can occur. Acknowledging one's fears and doubts can lead to breakthroughs in understanding and acceptance, paving the way for a renewed sense of purpose and strength.

Ultimately, the journey of a mother can mirror Hagar's narrative of resilience and hope. The weight of isolation may be heavy, but it does not define the entirety of one's experience. Just as Hagar emerged from the desert with renewed strength and a promise of future generations, modern women can find their path toward healing and empowerment. By reclaiming their stories and recognizing their inherent worth, mothers can transform their journeys into narratives of rebirth, proving that even in the wilderness of despair, growth and community are not only possible but essential.

Chapter Three

Struggling in the Desert - The Strength of a Woman and Mother

---

The desert without food or water is a brutal and unforgiving place. Extreme dehydration sets in bringing intense symptoms as the body struggles to cope without water. Initially, the mouth becomes very dry, making it difficult to swallow. The heart begins to race, and breathing becomes shallow as circulation strains under limited fluids, leading to headaches, dizziness, and even mental confusion. Painful muscle cramps develop due to imbalanced electrolytes, and skin becomes so dry and starts to crack. Nausea sets in, intensifying fluid loss, while thirst becomes overwhelming but can eventually fade as the body starts to shut down. Without intervention, Hagar and her son would not be able survive this extreme state of dehydration and severe disorientation, irritability, unconsciousness, and eventually death would be the result, as the body's systems fail without essential hydration.

Hagar has reached the end of her strength but never underestimate a mother. The strength of a mother in dire situations is a force that defies limits and rises from the depths of love, determination, and sacrifice. When faced with overwhelming hardship, a mother's strength is fierce and instinctive, born of an unwavering commitment to protect and provide for her children, no matter the cost to herself. It's the strength that drives her to find hope even in despair, to scrape together a sense of calm for her children when fear overtakes her own heart, and to push through physical exhaustion and pain when every fiber of her being begs her to rest. Hagar can no longer bear to watch as her son weakens and begins to die. She sets him under a shrub and retreats to a distance place opposite him, too overcome by her pain to witness his suffering, but she does not give up.

In this place of utter helplessness, Hagar's spirit does not wither. She lifts her face and cries out with every ounce of strength, as only a mother can, pouring every ounce of her anguish and longing into a plea for mercy. Her voice cracks, raspy from thirst, each syllable heavy with exhaustion and grief. She holds nothing back, her sobs shaking her frame, as if each one is drawn from the deepest part of her soul. It is the sound of helplessness, of a mother whose only wish is to protect her child yet who feels powerless to do so. This cry is not polished or practiced; it is unguarded, stripped of pretense, it is the raw cry of a mother who has given everything, who has carried all she could until she could bear it no longer. In her anguish, she doesn't try to control her emotions or pretend to be strong. Hagar's cry in the wilderness is the cry of a mother brought to the edge of despair. It rises up from the depths of her being. She simply lays bare her sorrow and helplessness, exposing the depths of her heart to the One she believes can still hear her. She has come to a place where words fail, and what remains is a sound - a primal, desperate wail that fills the empty desert air and pierces through the silence.

Chapter Four

Acknowledgement of the Marginalized - The Message of Comfort

It's in her darkest moment that her faith finds its voice, and her silent cry reaches heaven. In response, an angel appears, calling her by name and reminding her that she is seen, heard, and known. God has not forsaken her; He has remembered her and her child. In her vulnerability, she encounters God's presence not as a distant observer, but as the One who is intimately aware of her suffering. As an Egyptian servant and a single mother, Hagar's social status in the ancient world was very low. Her life and choices were largely controlled by others, and her needs and desires were often dismissed. Yet, God's appearance to her in the desert signifies that she is not just another servant or outsider; she is a person of value, seen and known by God Himself. This act of divine acknowledgment holds deep meaning for mothers today who may feel disregarded or unseen by their communities. God's revelation of care for her and her son becomes a source of inspiration for those seeking solace in their own struggles.

In desperate times, when burdens feel too heavy to bear alone, the simple act of someone acknowledging what you're feeling can make all the difference. In moments of pain, isolation, or overwhelming struggle, being truly seen by another provides a profound sense of relief and comfort. This recognition doesn't just validate the reality of your suffering–it offers an emotional anchor, a reminder that you are not invisible, that your experience has meaning and significance. This acknowledgement, especially in times of deep despair, is often the first step towards healing.

When someone else acknowledges our feelings, it sends a signal that our pain matters and that we are worthy of compassion and understanding. In the midst of darkness, people often feel isolated, as though their struggles are unique or misunderstood. Even if others cannot change the circumstances, simply recognizing and affirming the pain can ease the intense loneliness of suffering. This empathy can feel like a lifeline, providing the kind of companionship that says, "I may not be able to fix this, but I am here with you in it."

Acknowledgment also gives us permission to feel what we're feeling. Society sometimes places a heavy expectation on people to be strong, to "move on," or to "look on the bright side," especially in challenging situations. But for those who are struggling, this pressure to hide pain can be suffocating. The simple act of acknowledgment validates the complex reality of our feelings and offers a safe space for us to experience them without shame or judgment. This permission to feel fully can be incredibly liberating and healing, providing a sense of freedom that often allows people to begin processing their pain.

Furthermore, acknowledgment from others can help reframe and give language to experiences that feel too overwhelming to put into words. When someone articulates what they see in our suffering, it brings clarity to emotions that may feel chaotic, helping us understand ourselves better. It's as though they hold up a mirror that reflects our inner turmoil back to us in a way that makes it more comprehensible, more manageable. Through this process, people can begin to make sense of their experience and find the words they need to communicate their feelings, which is a vital step in processing trauma or hardship.

In desperate times, being seen and understood by another person rekindles hope and the possibility of resilience. When someone cares enough to acknowledge our pain, it reminds us that we have worth beyond our struggles. This recognition acts as a reminder that there is still light and compassion in the world, even in the darkest times. It offers hope that if one person can see and understand us, then perhaps we can find our way through this pain with support and love. It restores faith in human connection, providing a foundation upon which we can begin to rebuild.

Having someone acknowledge our experience can give us strength to move forward. Knowing that we are not carrying our burdens alone provides the courage to face difficulties with a renewed sense of resilience. It's not that acknowledgment removes the struggle itself, but it lightens the emotional load, making it easier to take each step. It strengthens our capacity to endure, empowering us to face even the hardest times with the reassurance that someone stands beside us, ready to listen and care.

The power of acknowledgment in desperate times cannot be overstated. It provides validation, connection, and relief from loneliness. It allows us to fully feel and understand our pain, and ultimately gives us strength and hope to carry on. When someone takes the time to see and honor our experience, it can transform our journey through hardship, offering comfort that endures long after the moment of acknowledgment has passed. The wilderness, once a place of desolation, transforms into a space of healing and growth, where we can find strength in vulnerabilities and emerge with renewed purpose, ready to embrace the challenges ahead with courage and hope.

One of the most hopeful moments in Hagar's story is when, in the depths of despair in the desert, God provides a well of water to sustain her and her son. At her lowest point, Hagar believes she has reached the end, unable to bear the sight of her child's suffering. God's provision of water symbolizes hope and sustenance, a source of support that arrives at the very moment she feels she cannot go on. This divine act of provision is profoundly encouraging for mothers today who face the daunting task of providing for their children, often with limited resources and little support.

Additionally, God's promise that her son will become the father of a great nation speaks to the future and potential for her generations. This divine assurance is profoundly comforting, suggesting that her generation is destined for greatness, not limited by their present circumstances or defined by the absence of a father. For mothers, Hagar's story offers hope that their children have a bright future, filled with potential and purpose, and that their efforts as mothers are instrumental in shaping that future. This promise reassures mothers that, despite the challenges, their children's futures are in good hands and that their love and dedication will help pave the way for their children's success and fulfillment.

Chapter Five

Finding the Well of Water Within – Cultivating Inner Resources

In every woman's heart, there is a well of living water - a deep, nourishing source of strength, wisdom, and grace that has the power to sustain her through life's most demanding seasons. This well is not external; it is internal, a place where a woman can draw from when she feels weary, overwhelmed, or disconnected from herself. Yet, often, in the hustle of daily life, the well can feel hidden, buried beneath layers of responsibilities, expectations, and emotional exhaustion. The journey of finding this well is not a one-time event, but rather a process of returning to it, remembering it, and learning how to draw from it again and again.

This chapter is an exploration of how women can discover, reconnect with, and cultivate the deep well of resources that lies within them. It is a reminder that the strength to face the challenges of life, the wisdom to make decisions, and the peace to navigate uncertainty are all within reach, even when it feels as though they are distant or absent.

A well is a symbol of depth and sustenance. In ancient times, wells were essential sources of life. They provided water not only for drinking but for washing, cooking, and sustaining livestock. The well was the center of community life, a place where people gathered, shared, and found the resources needed to survive. In a similar way, the well within a woman is a source of emotional, spiritual, and psychological nourishment that can restore her when she is feeling drained or disconnected.

For many women, finding this well requires a process of inner exploration—a journey into the depths of their own heart and soul. Life's demands can easily drown out the voice of intuition, and the noise of societal pressures can cloud a woman's sense of self. The constant juggling of responsibilities—whether as a mother, partner, or professional—can leave little room for self-reflection or emotional replenishment. In these moments, the well may seem elusive, but it is always there, waiting to be rediscovered.

The angel of the Lord appears to Hagar and speaks directly to her, offering guidance and a promise. This moment is pivotal in her spiritual journey. The God who sees her, who notices her plight, and who intervenes in her situation, is the same God who reveals that there is a well of water even in the desert - a symbol of divine provision. Hagar's encounter with the well becomes a metaphor for finding the divine presence within our own hearts—a wellspring of peace, strength, wisdom, and faith that we can draw upon in times of need. This well does not rely on external circumstances or human relationships but is found by cultivating a deeper relationship with the divine presence that sustains us.

Just as Hagar was forced to confront her own vulnerability and despair in the desert, modern women too must face their own brokenness in order to discover the living water that is already within. To find the well within, one must first acknowledge the wilderness - the times of struggle, loneliness, and despair. It is in these moments of difficulty that women are most likely to search inwardly for the strength needed to continue. Inner strength is not about being invincible or never feeling overwhelmed; rather, it is the ability to tap into a sense of resilience and purpose when facing adversity. For a woman and mother, inner strength often comes from the recognition that her worth is not tied to perfection but to her ability to continue growing, learning, and responding with love, even in the face of difficulties.

The well within is not only a metaphor for strength; it is also a wellspring of peace, healing, and creativity. It is a place of spiritual connection, where a woman can return to the essence of who she is and remember her innate worth. It is where she finds clarity during confusion, renewal when exhausted, and perspective when overwhelmed. The well is both a resource and a reminder—reminding her of her own power, her own worth, and her capacity to navigate life with grace.

The process of finding the well begins with the journey inward. This requires intentionality and a willingness to pause. It is in the stillness of silence, in moments of reflection, that a woman can begin to reconnect with herself and uncover the well of strength that has always been there. However, in the business of life, this stillness is often the first thing to be sacrificed. The constant demands of work, family, and social expectations can leave little room for personal reflection or soul-nourishment.

One of the first steps in rediscovering the well within is creating space for silence. This does not necessarily mean hours of quiet or solitude (though those can certainly help), but it means intentionally carving out moments in each day to simply be with oneself. This could be a few minutes of breathing exercises in the morning before the world starts, a walk in nature, a journal entry, or a prayerful pause during the day. In these moments, a woman can reflect on her own emotional and spiritual needs, checking in with herself and listening to the deeper voice within.

As she begins this process of introspection, a woman may discover areas of her life where she feels drained or disconnected. Perhaps there is a pattern of self-neglect, an unspoken desire for rest, or a longing for deeper connection with her own heart. This awareness is the first step in reclaiming the well—recognizing that there is a place inside of her that has been overlooked or undernourished. It is in these moments of self-awareness that a woman can begin to shift from external dependence to internal reliance, learning to trust the well within her to provide what she needs.

Once the well is rediscovered, the next step is nurturing it - taking the time and effort to cultivate the internal resources that will sustain a woman through life's inevitable ups and downs. This process involves developing practices that replenish her energy, support her emotional health, and nurture her spirit.

This process often involves a form of surrender, an acknowledgment that we cannot rely on our own strength alone but must tap into a higher power, a source of divine grace. It involves self-awareness, self-compassion and self-care.

The well within can be seen as a symbol of spiritual practices that help us reconnect with the divine. Prayer, meditation, scripture reading, and moments of quiet reflection all help to deepen our awareness of the presence of God. These practices serve as ways to "dig" deeper into our own hearts and souls, to access the wellspring of strength and peace that God has placed within us. Just as Hagar experienced renewal through her encounter with the divine, so too can women experience moments of spiritual renewal that restore the soul and provide the energy and direction needed to move forward. It is often when women feel most desperate that the well of water within becomes most accessible—when we are emptied of self-reliance, we become open to receiving the spiritual nourishment we need.

Many women find a profound sense of inner strength and resources through their spiritual practices. Whether a woman is religious or spiritual in nature, the connection to something greater than herself can provide a source of strength and peace that transcends daily challenges. For mothers, spiritual strength offers a foundation on which to build resilience.

Spiritual practices such as prayer, meditation, journaling, or simply spending time in nature can help women center themselves and access a sense of peace amidst the chaos of daily life. These practices provide a space for reflection, a time to reconnect with one's deeper sense of purpose and identity beyond the roles of woman and mother. Spirituality also offers a source of hope, helping mothers to keep perspective during difficult moments and to feel a sense of connection to the divine or to something bigger than their immediate circumstances.

For many, faith in a higher power provides both comfort and guidance. It can offer a sense of purpose and a reminder that even in the hardest moments, there is meaning and a broader plan at work. Spiritual strength is often built through times of adversity, as women lean into their faith for the courage to keep going, trusting that their efforts are seen and valued.

Even without a formal religious framework, the practice of mindfulness—being present in the moment without judgment—can serve as a powerful tool for nurturing inner strength. This practice encourages women to quiet the mental chatter that often accompanies stress and anxiety, helping them to reframe challenges and approach them with a calm, centered mindset.

One of the most important steps toward finding inner strength is cultivating self-awareness. When a woman becomes a mother, she may find herself so consumed with the needs of her children that she loses touch with her own identity, desires, and needs. A key aspect of rediscovering inner strength is learning to reconnect with oneself—not as just a mother, but as a person with unique talents, aspirations, and emotions.

Self-awareness involves taking time to reflect on one's emotions, needs, and limits. It means acknowledging when you are struggling, when you need support, and when you are feeling drained. By recognizing these signs, a woman can better understand what resources—whether emotional, physical, or spiritual—she needs to replenish herself. Self-awareness also allows mothers to set realistic expectations for themselves, recognizing that they cannot do everything at once and that it is okay to ask for help or take a step back when needed.

Along with self-awareness comes self-compassion - the practice of treating oneself with the same kindness and understanding that one would offer to a loved one. Motherhood is full of moments of imperfection, and the pressures to "do it all" can lead to harsh self-judgment. But finding inner strength requires a shift in perspective: recognizing that mistakes and challenges are part of the human experience and being gentle with oneself in the face of them. Self-compassion allows a woman to embrace her imperfections, knowing that she is doing the best she can in a constantly evolving role. This compassion nurtures resilience, as it fosters the emotional space to recover from setbacks and move forward with renewed energy.

While self-awareness and self-compassion are important, another crucial component of finding inner strength is self-care. It's easy for mothers, especially those who juggle multiple responsibilities, to neglect their own well-being in favor of caring for others. However, self-care is not a luxury; it is a necessity for long-term physical, emotional, and mental health.

Self-care can take many forms - whether it's getting enough sleep, exercising, eating nutritious food, taking time for hobbies, or simply spending a quiet moment alone. When mothers take the time to care for themselves, they are better equipped to care for their families. Just as an airplane safety demonstration reminds passengers to put on their own oxygen mask before helping others, mothers must prioritize their own well-being in order to be truly present for their children.

Self-care is also about recognizing the importance of setting boundaries. Women must learn to say no when necessary, to protect their time and energy for the things that truly matter. This may involve asking for help with household tasks, setting aside time each day for personal reflection, or taking breaks from the pressures of motherhood.

Small, consistent acts of self-care can make all the difference.

- Physical care: Exercise, eat nourishing foods, drink water, and get enough sleep. When we take care of our bodies, our minds and spirits follow suit.
- Emotional care: Talk to a friend, join a support group, or seek counseling when needed. Don't be afraid to ask for help when you need it.
- Mental care: Read a book for pleasure, engage in a hobby, or learn something new. Mental stimulation that is separate from your daily responsibilities can help clear your mind.
- Spiritual care: Whether it's through prayer, attending religious services, or connecting with nature, nourish your soul in ways that give you a sense of peace and grounding.

Being present in the moment is another powerful practice for reconnecting with the well within. In the midst of busy lives, it is easy to become distracted or disconnected from what truly matters. Mindfulness is the practice of bringing one's full attention to the present moment, whether that's savoring a quiet cup of tea, listening intently to a loved one, or simply sitting with one's thoughts.

Mindfulness helps a woman slow down, breathe, and reconnect with her inner world. By cultivating mindfulness, she can create a space of calm amidst the noise, allowing her to draw on the well within for clarity and peace. In these moments of presence, the well is accessed and replenished, offering her the emotional grounding needed to face whatever challenges lie ahead.

The well within is not just a source of strength to be drawn upon in times of need; it is also a source of power and transformation. When a woman taps into her inner well, she can move beyond mere survival and begin to thrive. The well within is a place where creativity flows, where new ideas are born, and where a woman's unique gifts and talents come alive.

As a woman nurtures her well, she begins to see herself not just as a caretaker or responder to life's demands, but as a co-creator of her own reality. She realizes that her well is not only for her own replenishment but for the benefit of others. The more deeply she draws from the well within, the more she has to offer the world.

The well is a source of transformation because it empowers a woman to change her mindset, release limiting beliefs, and step into her true potential. By trusting the well, a woman finds the courage to pursue her dreams, take risks, and embrace new opportunities. The well is a place of rebirth, where she can shed old patterns and beliefs that no longer serve her, emerging stronger and more aligned with her authentic self.

Finding the well of water within is not a destination, but a continuous journey of self-discovery, self-care, and spiritual nourishment. It is an ongoing process of reconnecting with the depth of one's own heart and soul, cultivating inner strength, and drawing from the well when life becomes overwhelming.

Every woman has access to this well, regardless of her circumstances, and when she learns to tap into its resources, she finds herself transformed. The well within offers not only the strength to survive, but the power to thrive and create a life of meaning, purpose, and joy.

As you journey through life, remember that the well is always there.

Chapter Six

Seeking Community - The Quest for Belonging

In the vast expanse of life's challenges, the quest for belonging often feels like a solitary journey, especially for mothers navigating their unique landscapes of adversity. As they manage their responsibilities alone, they can feel overwhelmed by the weight of their challenges. This sense of isolation can be amplified by societal judgments and misconceptions about motherhood, and especially single motherhood, creating barriers that make it difficult to forge meaningful relationships. The desire for belonging becomes not just a wish but a necessity for emotional survival, as community and support can provide the solace needed to navigate the tumultuous waters of parenting.

The generational struggles faced by mothers often mirror those of Hagar, whose story speaks to the cyclical nature of hardship and resilience. Each woman's journey is unique, yet the threads of sacrifice, hope, and survival connect their narratives. Just as Hagar was compelled to find a way to nurture her son in the face of despair, modern mothers are driven by an unwavering love for their children, propelling them to seek out communities that understand their plight. This search is not merely about finding a support system; it is about reclaiming their identity and strengthening the bonds that will empower future generations.

Faith plays a crucial role in this quest for belonging, often serving as both a refuge and a source of doubt. Mothers may wrestle with their beliefs, questioning their purpose and the presence of a higher power in their struggles. Hagar's encounter with God in the wilderness highlights the transformative power of faith, reminding women that their spiritual journey can lead to profound revelations. This interplay between faith and doubt can ultimately foster a deeper sense of belonging, as women find solace in shared beliefs and experiences within their communities.

In addition to faith, establishing connections with other women who share similar experiences can be a powerful antidote to the loneliness that often accompanies motherhood. Support networks can take many forms, from formal groups to casual friendships. These relationships provide not only emotional support but also practical assistance in navigating the challenges of parenting alone. Sharing the burdens of daily life with others who understand the weight of those struggles can foster a sense of belonging and validation, reminding us that we are not alone in our journey.

As we seek to build these networks, it is essential to approach the process with openness and vulnerability. Just as Hagar displayed courage and strength in the face of adversity, we too must embrace our own vulnerabilities to connect authentically with others. Sharing our stories, our fears, and our triumphs creates a space where mutual support can flourish. This openness can lead to meaningful friendships that become lifelines in moments of despair, reminding us that we have allies in our quest for healing and growth.

Ultimately, the journey of a mother is not just about survival; it is about rebirth in the wilderness. Each connection we foster within our support networks contributes to our emotional landscape, allowing us to heal and grow. As we navigate the complexities of faith and doubt, we can find strength in the stories we share and the bonds we create. By embracing the power of community and the richness of our narratives, we step into a new chapter of our lives, one where we are not only surviving but thriving in the embrace of solidarity and love.

Chapter Seven

Speaking into the Future

The act of speaking into the future is both an ancient and deeply spiritual practice. In the Bible, words are not only seen as tools of communication but as instruments of power and creation. From the very beginning, the Bible presents words as powerful agents of creation. In Genesis 1:3, God speaks the world into existence: *"And God said, 'Let there be light,' and there was light."* Words were not merely descriptive; they were formative. In Proverbs 18:21, we are reminded that *"death and life are in the power of the tongue, and those who love it will eat its fruit."* This verse underscores the biblical truth that our words are not neutral—they carry weight and have the potential to either build up or tear down.

Hagar's story offers us deep insight into how a woman, too, can speak words of affirmation into her life. Just as God gave Hagar a vision of her future that was far bigger than herself, similarly, a woman can affirm that her life, though sometimes difficult, is part of a greater, eternal plan. Women are playing a role in God's story, and this has a far-reaching impact, not just for each woman but for generations to come. God calls women to declare His truth over their circumstances, identities, and the futures of loved ones. In Mark 11:24, Jesus said *"Therefore I say to you, whatever things you ask when you pray, believe that you receive them, and you will have them."*

We all have an inner dialogue, and for many women, that inner voice can be critical and self-deprecating. Negative self-talk can rob us of our joy and confidence. The internal dialogue shapes thoughts, which shape actions, which ultimately shape lives. When women continually speak words of negativity or doubt to themselves, they limit their potential. Speaking biblical affirmations helps to replace lies and doubts with truth, gradually shifting our mindset from defeat to victory. But when we speak life-affirming, faith-filled words, we align ourselves with God's truth and open the door to the abundant life He promises.

Positive affirmations are not about conjuring up unrealistic ideals or affirming things that aren't true. Rather, they are about aligning our words with the truth of who God says we are and speaking His promises into our hearts and our circumstances. When we declare God's truth over our lives, we are not only affirming our identity in Him, but we are also creating an environment for growth, healing, and peace.

When life gets busy or difficult, it's easy to forget who you truly are. In the roles of wife, mother, worker, and friend, you may lose sight of your personal identity. Affirmations rooted in Scripture remind you that your identity is not based on your performance or circumstances but on who you are in Christ. You are a beloved daughter of God, and your value is secure in Him.

Speaking positive affirmations bolsters your confidence. It empowers you to step forward with courage, knowing that you are equipped and called for the tasks before you. When you declare God's truth over your life, you are acknowledging that His strength, His wisdom, and His presence are with you every step of the way. This gives you the courage to tackle challenges with a sense of purpose and faith.

Affirmations help to shift your focus from what is lacking to what is good. When you regularly declare God's promises and blessings, your heart becomes more attuned to gratitude. In turn, this fosters joy, even in the midst of trials. Philippians 4:8 encourages us to think about whatever is true, noble, right, pure, lovely, and admirable - things that are worthy of praise. Affirmations help us to align our thoughts with this mindset, creating a heart of peace and thankfulness.

No matter how small or large your daily tasks seem, remember that they are significant. You are shaping the next generation with your love, prayers, and guidance. Speaking affirmations like, "I am doing important work," helps to frame your daily efforts as part of God's greater plan for your family.

When you speak affirmations of confidence and self-love, you are modeling for your children what it looks like to walk in God's truth. Your words will shape their understanding of self-worth, identity, and faith. As you speak life into your own heart, you're also sowing seeds of life into theirs.

One of the most profound ways a mother can speak into the future is by speaking life into her children. When we speak with purpose, with faith, and with an understanding of our role in God's plan, we are creating a legacy of hope and truth for those who come after us. The words we speak into the future are part of God's greater narrative—a narrative that transcends time and reaches beyond our own lives.

Ultimately, speaking into the future as a woman or mother is rooted in faith. It's the faith that God's promises are true, that He will provide, and that His plans for our lives and the lives of our children are good. It's the faith that we can trust God with our families, our futures, and our words.

In Jeremiah 29:11, God declares, *"For I know the plans I have for you, declares the Lord, plans for welfare and not for evil, to give you a future and a hope."* These words are just as true for us today as they were for the Israelites. When we speak life, when we pray, and when we declare God's truth over our lives and the lives of our children, we are aligning ourselves with His good plans for the future.

Here are some key affirmations we can take from Hagar's story and speak into our own lives, particularly when we feel burdened or uncertain about the future:

1. "God sees me, and He is with me."

   Just as God found Hagar in the desert, He sees us in our pain, confusion, or isolation. We are never forgotten or invisible to God. When we declare, "God sees me, and He is with me," we remind ourselves that God's presence is our constant source of strength, even in the wilderness of life.

2. "My future is not defined by my current circumstances."

   In the wilderness, Hagar's immediate reality was full of hardship. Yet, God spoke a promise over her future, a future that would be filled with blessing. As we speak this affirmation, we choose to believe that our present struggles are temporary, and that God has a future full of hope and purpose for us and our families.

3. "I am not alone—God is guiding my steps."

   Hagar was not just given a promise. God didn't abandon her to figure things out on her own; He gave her direction. In the same way, we can declare, "God is guiding my steps," even when the path forward is unclear. We trust that He will show us where to go and lead us through every season.

4. "I am a part of God's bigger plan."

   When God spoke to Hagar, He gave her a glimpse into a future that was far bigger than herself—her descendants would become a great nation. Similarly, we can affirm that our lives, though sometimes difficult, are part of a greater, eternal plan. We are playing a role in God's story, and our lives have a far-reaching impact, not just for ourselves but for generations to come.

5. "My children have a future filled with purpose and promise."

   Hagar's son, Ishmael, was promised to become the father of a great nation. As mothers, we can declare over our children that their future is not one of hopelessness, but of divine purpose. Despite challenges, we speak life and hope into their futures, trusting that God has a plan for each of them.

Chapter Eight

Reclaiming the Narrative - Write Your Own Story

In a world where the narratives of women often go unheard, it is essential to reclaim and rewrite these stories. The tale of Hagar and Ishmael in the desert serves as a poignant metaphor for the struggles and triumphs faced by mothers today. Hagar, cast out and alone, embodies the isolation that many women experience when navigating the complexities of motherhood without support. Her journey through the barren landscape mirrors the emotional deserts that mother's traverse—places of despair, doubt, and longing for connection. By reflecting on Hagar's story, we can find solace and inspiration to pen our own narratives, transforming feelings of abandonment into tales of resilience.

Writing one's own story as a woman is an empowering, transformative act that allows her to reclaim her voice, define her identity, and assert her place in the world. In a world where women's experiences are often filtered through others' perceptions, writing one's story is a bold act of self-expression, an opportunity to shape her narrative on her terms. She can start by reflecting on her journey of her hardship, delving into her memories, confronting her challenges, and celebrating her victories. By reflecting on her journey, she can begin to understand her resilience, seeing the ways she has endured and survived. Reclaiming her life involves setting new goals or rediscovering old dreams, focusing on what she wants rather than what she has endured. She can rebuild her sense of self by exploring her passions, finding activities that bring her joy and fulfillment, and establishing boundaries that protect her well-being. Surrounding herself with supportive people who uplift her can be transformative, as they remind her of her worth and potential. With time and patience, she can redefine herself not by the hardships she has faced, but by the strength, wisdom, and compassion she has gained through them, embracing her right to live fully, joyfully, and on her own terms. By taking control of her story, she not only honors her unique experiences but also paves the way for others to connect with their own stories.

Writing her story can involve revisiting intimate, vulnerable, or painful moments, and it's essential to allow herself to feel what she feels. She doesn't need to have everything figured out from the start. It's important for her to resist the urge to "polish" her story or make it conform to others' expectations. Authenticity is key; it is her truth that gives her story power. Her voice, her language, and her perspective should shine through, regardless of how different or unusual they may seem to others. Her life may not fit the stereotypical image of success or perfection, but it is real, and that authenticity is what resonates most deeply.

As she reclaims her life, it's helpful to embrace the different facets of her identity that have shaped her experience. Each role she has played—daughter, sister, partner, mother, friend, or professional—holds its own unique stories and struggles, and each is a vital part of her whole self. By weaving together these different threads, she creates a more complete and nuanced portrait of who she is. Her story doesn't have to follow a linear path; it can meander, capture multiple perspectives, or even focus on specific themes that define her experiences. She has the freedom to explore her identity from every angle, allowing her to see her own complexity and honor the various ways she has grown and evolved. She can confront moments when she felt marginalized, misunderstood, or unseen, and she can redefine them on her terms. She can give voice to parts of herself that may have been silenced or hidden, bringing them to light with compassion and courage. This process of facing and owning her past can be incredibly healing, as it allows her to find closure, gain insight, and sometimes even find forgiveness for herself and others.

Chapter Nine

The Permission to Love and Be Loved Again

In the wilderness, Hagar receives not just a revelation of God's love for her but also a transformative understanding of how she might come to love again. She was no longer just the servant; she was a woman whose life had meaning, whose future was secure, and whose heart could be healed from the wounds of neglect. Through God's intervention, Hagar learns that love is not contingent on human validation, but rather on divine affirmation. Even in the midst of suffering, God's love does not abandon her; it compels her to move forward with a renewed sense of self.

Love is one of the most profound and transformative experiences a person can undergo. It has the power to heal, to uplift, and to bring immense joy. Yet, for many women love can also bring pain, heartache, and loss. After such experiences, the ability to love and to be loved again may feel uncertain or even unattainable. The journey of granting oneself permission to love again, whether it is after the end of a relationship, the loss of a loved one, or emotional injury, can be a complex, daunting process. Yet, it is one of the most vital steps toward emotional recovery and personal growth.

For those who have experienced deep emotional wounds, the idea of opening oneself to love again can seem impossible. Love, in its most vulnerable form, demands trust, intimacy, and emotional investment, elements that can feel perilous after one has been hurt. The scars left by betrayal, rejection, or loss often create a protective shell around the heart, causing individuals to resist the idea of future affection. The fear of suffering once more can lead to emotional shutdowns or an unconscious decision to close off from the potential of new relationships.

This emotional hesitation is a natural defense mechanism, a way of protecting oneself from further pain. However, it is also a trap. It can lead to isolation, loneliness, and the belief that love is no longer for us. In reality, this fear often stems from the past, and the experiences that shaped it may not dictate the future.

Therefore, the first step toward granting oneself permission to love again involves recognizing the weight of past hurts and acknowledging that these experiences do not have to define our capacity for love in the future.

Healing from emotional wounds is neither linear nor swift. It requires time, self-compassion, and a willingness to confront the pain head-on. In the aftermath of loss or betrayal, it can be difficult to distinguish between the person who was hurt and the person who is capable of healing. Yet, healing involves reframing one's narrative. It means understanding that while the past has shaped us, it does not have to limit us.

Self-love is often the foundation upon which the permission to love others is built. When a person learns to care for and accept themselves, flaws, scars, and all, they become better equipped to welcome love in all its forms. This involves cultivating patience with oneself and seeking out practices that promote mental and emotional well-being, such as mindfulness, therapy, or healthy social connections. Only through this inner healing can a person regain the ability to trust both themselves and others again, which is essential for new bonds to form.

Granting oneself permission to love again requires courage. It is not a decision made lightly but one that comes with the realization that the potential for future happiness and connection is worth the risk of vulnerability. To open oneself to love means allowing the possibility of both joy and sorrow. This is the paradox of love; it is both the source of our greatest pleasures and sometimes our greatest pains. Yet, it is through embracing both the risks and rewards that we grow emotionally and learn more about ourselves and others.

Courage in love is not about ignoring fear or the past; it is about accepting that fear is part of the journey. It is about choosing to trust again, despite the pain of what has come before. It is about allowing oneself to feel, to connect, and to be present in new relationships without the shadow of past trauma dictating every action and thought.

A critical component of the permission to love again is the ability to trust, both in others and in oneself. Trust is not a switch that can be flipped overnight, especially after it has been broken. However, trust is something that can be rebuilt slowly, over time, through consistent actions and a willingness to be vulnerable. In the beginning, it might seem easier to withhold trust, to hold back emotionally, but the only way to truly experience the depth and beauty of love is through full engagement. When we trust, we allow ourselves to experience both the joy of connection and the possibility of vulnerability.

Moreover, trusting oneself is equally important. The decision to love again is an act of self-empowerment. It is the acknowledgment that, despite past experiences, we have the emotional resilience to navigate future relationships. It is about knowing that we are capable of making wise choices, protecting ourselves when necessary, and learning from every encounter.

When the walls built by past heartache begin to crumble, and a person permits themselves to love and be loved again, they open themselves to an entirely new chapter of life. Love, in its many forms, is not a finite resource, it is an abundant force that can continue to grow and evolve. Each new relationship or connection carries the potential for joy, growth, and mutual respect. And even when love leads to loss again, the experience still holds value. Through the act of loving and being loved, we learn more about ourselves, develop empathy, and discover new capacities for connection.

In allowing ourselves to love again, we affirm our belief in the goodness of the world, in the possibility of new beginnings, and in the power of human connection. It is a testament to the resilience of the human spirit that, despite the pain of the past, we can choose to open our hearts to the future.

The permission to love and be loved again is not something granted by others; it is a gift we give ourselves. It requires time, healing, courage, and trust. But it is also a source of great reward. When we open ourselves to love again, we allow ourselves to experience the fullness of life, with all its beauty, vulnerability, and connection. By embracing the opportunity to love again, we affirm our capacity for growth, healing, and joy, and we come to understand that love is not only a bond with others but an act of profound self-affirmation.

Chapter Ten

Finding Rest and Peace

The life of a woman and mother is often a delicate balancing act, constantly shifting between roles, responsibilities, and relationships. In the midst of nurturing children, managing a household, working, and tending to personal needs, finding true rest and peace can feel like a distant dream. Yet, it's possible to cultivate a sense of calm amidst the chaos—though it requires intentionality, patience, and a deep understanding of what rest truly means.

One of the first steps toward finding rest is letting go of the myth of perfection. In our fast-paced, image-driven society, women are often bombarded with messages that they should excel in every area of life: work, home, fitness, parenting, social life, and even spirituality. The pressure to "do it all" perfectly can leave little room for the quiet, replenishing peace we so desperately need.

Rest doesn't mean doing less; it means doing less with more intention. It's about surrendering to the reality that perfection is unattainable, and instead focusing on progress, grace, and the acceptance that imperfection is part of the human experience. Embracing imperfection allows us to stop constantly striving and start finding peace in the here and now.

Women are often conditioned to prioritize others over themselves. This deep sense of responsibility to families and communities can leave them emotionally and physically drained. However, in order to pour into others, women must first be filled. Rest starts within, and it begins by tuning into your own body, mind, and soul.

This requires listening to your needs without guilt or shame. A simple act of mindfulness - whether it's pausing for a few deep breaths, journaling your thoughts, or practicing meditation - can help you reconnect with your inner self. Understanding what you need in any given moment is the first step toward carving out space for rest. Is it physical rest? Emotional rest? Creative rest? Spiritual rest? Once you begin to identify the areas where you're feeling drained, you can take steps to nourish those parts of you.

When most people think of rest, they think of sleep. And while sleep is vital to our well-being, rest is much more than simply getting enough hours of shut-eye. True rest involves rejuvenating the body, calming the mind, and soothing the spirit. It is a holistic experience that nurtures every part of who you are.

Consider rest as a series of small practices throughout your day that allow you to recharge. It may be as simple as:

- A cup of tea in silence: Take five minutes each morning or afternoon to simply sit and drink your tea. No phone, no distractions - just a quiet moment to center yourself.
- A mindful walk: Walking outdoors is an act of grounding. Breathe in the fresh air, notice the beauty around you, and let go of the thoughts that race through your mind. It's a brief reset, but it can have profound benefits for your peace of mind.
- Creative outlets: Whether it's painting, writing, knitting, or gardening, creative expression is a powerful form of rest. It allows you to get out of your head and into your body, freeing you from the weight of daily concerns.
- Prayer or meditation: If you're spiritually inclined, prayer or meditation offers an opportunity to release

your burdens and find solace in something greater than yourself.

It's also important to remember that rest can take many forms, and the key is variety. Different days may require different types of rest, depending on what you're feeling and experiencing. On some days, you may need a long bath, while on others, an afternoon nap may be what restores you. Pay attention to what you're craving and honor those needs.

For many women, well-being is an afterthought - something that only happens if all other responsibilities have been met. But in order to truly rest and find peace, we must prioritize our well-being, just as we prioritize the needs of others. This doesn't mean you have to go on a week-long retreat (though that can be lovely!).

Your physical environment plays a huge role in your inner peace. A cluttered, disorganized space can often contribute to feelings of overwhelm and stress. While it's not realistic to have a perfectly clean home all the time, creating an environment that feels peaceful and intentional can have a powerful impact on your sense of well-being.

Simple changes like reducing clutter, creating designated areas for rest (such as a reading nook or a cozy corner), and keeping your space free from constant distractions can help foster a sense of tranquility. It's not about perfection; it's about creating a space that allows you to feel calm and present.

Rest and peace are not one-time accomplishments but ongoing practices that must be woven into the fabric of our daily lives. Just as the seasons change, so too will our need for rest ebb and flow. There will be seasons of busy, active mothering and seasons of quiet reflection and renewal. What matters is that we honor both and find a rhythm that allows us to honor our own needs while still caring for those we love.

Motherhood, like life, is a marathon, not a sprint. If women try to do everything all at once, they will burn out. But when we build in moments of rest—when we let go of unrealistic expectations and learn to nurture oneselves as much as we nurture others—we open ourselves to the possibility of true peace.

In the midst of the demands of motherhood and life, it's essential to remember that rest isn't a luxury - it's a necessity. It's not something we should feel guilty about; it's the foundation for all the love, care, and strength we offer. By finding rest and peace, we not only heal ourselves but also create a more peaceful, loving environment for those we care about.

Chapter Eleven

Inspirational Stories of Ten Women Who Rewrote Their Stories

Throughout history, countless women have faced unimaginable hardship, yet they found ways to rewrite their narratives and rise from the challenges they endured. Their stories are filled with resilience, courage, and a deep-seated determination to create something meaningful from their pain. These women not only changed their lives but also inspired and empowered others to overcome their struggles. Here are the inspirational stories of some everyday women who faced extreme hardship but rewrote their stories

Melissa Kieling: Personal need to Business Idea

Melissa Kieling is a successful entrepreneur and the founder of Packit, a company that created the first freezable, foldable bag to keep food and drinks cool without the need for ice packs. Her journey to launching PackIt is a story of resilience, creativity, and seizing an opportunity born from personal need.

Kieling's idea for PackIt came from her experience as a mother trying to pack healthy lunches for her three children. As a single mother going through a difficult divorce, she noticed her kids' lunch bags didn't keep food fresh by the time they were ready to eat, especially on hot days. She realized that traditional lunch bags, which required ice packs, were not efficient because the ice would melt quickly, often leaving food soggy and warm by lunchtime.

Determined to solve this problem, Kieling came up with the concept of a bag with built-in cooling technology. The bag itself would have freezable gel permanently sewn into its lining, allowing it to stay cold for hours after freezing. This unique design would keep food fresh without needing additional ice packs. Realizing that the solution to her personal need could benefit many others, Kieling turned this into a business idea.

Kieling initially funded her business by selling her own belongings and maxing out her credit cards. Under Kieling's leadership, PackIt grew into a successful business with a variety of products, from lunch bags to wine coolers and picnic bags. Her story has inspired many, especially women entrepreneurs, showing how personal challenges can fuel innovative solutions and lead to business success.

Madam C.J. Walker: Daughter of Slaves to First U.S. Female Self-Made Millionaire

Madam C.J. Walker was the first child in her family born into freedom. Orphaned by age 7 and a widow by age 20, she endured poverty and struggled to support herself and her daughter. She only had three months of formal education After the death of her parents, she went to live with her older sister where she was abused by her brother-in-law. In order to escape the abuse, she got married at the age of 14. Five years into the marriage her first husband died. Her venture into the hair care products business initially included selling hair care products as a job. She later developed and marketed her own line of hair care products for Black women, building a business empire and becoming the first female self-made millionaire in the U.S on record. She used her wealth to support social causes and became a prominent philanthropist.

Frida Kahlo: Trauma into Art

Frida Kahlo was a world renown Mexican artist, who turned her pain into Art. She faced health challenges from a young age, including polio, which left her with a lifelong limp. Despite this, she was a passionate and determined individual, excelling in her studies.

At the age of 18, Kahlo was involved in a severe bus accident that resulted in numerous injuries, including a broken spinal column, ribs, and pelvis. During her long recovery, she began to paint, often using a specially designed easel that allowed her to paint while lying down. This period marked the beginning of her artistic journey, and she started creating self-portraits, exploring themes of identity, pain, and the female experience. She created around 200 paintings, with about 55 being self-portraits. Kahlo was one of the few female artists to gain recognition during her lifetime, especially in Mexico and the U.S.

Oprah Winfrey: Poverty to Billionaire

Born to a single teenage mother and into extreme poverty in rural Mississippi, Oprah Winfrey faced a turbulent childhood marked by abuse, teenage pregnancy, instability, and hardship. After birth Oprah was left with her grandmother. Raised by her grandmother for part of her early years, she wore dresses made from potato sacks and dealt with physical and emotional hardships. By age

13, she had endured significant trauma, including abuse and neglect and became pregnant at the age of 14. Her son was born prematurely and died in infancy. After running away from home, she was sent to live with her father in Nashville, Tennessee, which proved to be a turning point. Her father instilled in her the value of education, discipline, and self-respect, setting her on a path toward change.

She channeled her passion and resilience into academics and public speaking, eventually earning a scholarship to Tennessee State University. Her breakthrough came in television, where her charismatic personality quickly propelled her to national fame. She redefined the talk-show genre, using her platform to inspire millions. Today, she's not only one of the wealthiest women in media but also a powerful advocate for education, mental health, and social change.

Cathy Hughes: Teenage mother to Media Mogul

Cathy Hughes' journey is a testament to resilience and vision. Born in Omaha, Nebraska, Hughes faced challenges early, becoming a teenage mother and experiencing homelessness. Determined to create a career in media, she worked her way up, eventually launching the radio station WOL in Washington, D.C., in 1980. Facing financial struggles, she persevered, later founding Radio One, a media company dedicated to serving Black audiences. Hughes became the first Black woman to lead a publicly traded company, building a media empire that now includes television network TV One.

Joy Mangano: Financial Struggle to Innovative Solutions

Joy Mangano's story is one of perseverance and ingenuity. As a single mother of three, Mangano struggled financially, working multiple jobs to support her family. In 1990, inspired by the difficulties of household cleaning, she invented the self-wringing "Miracle Mop." Facing initial rejections, Mangano eventually secured a slot on QVC, where she personally demonstrated her product and saw immediate success. Her product's popularity led to more inventions, like Huggable Hangers, and she became a leading personality on the Home Shopping Network (HSN).

Harriet Tubman: Slavery to Underground Railroad Hero

Harriet Tubman's life was marked by unimaginable hardship, but she emerged as one of the most remarkable figures in American history. Born into slavery, Tubman suffered abuse, physical trauma, and the constant threat of being sold away from her family. At the age of 29, she escaped to freedom, making the daring journey to the North.

However, she didn't stop there. Tubman became a leader of the Underground Railroad, risking her life to help hundreds of slaves escape to freedom. Over the course of her lifetime, she risked her life nineteen times to lead others to safety.

Her courage and commitment to justice and freedom made her a key figure in the abolitionist movement and in the fight for women's rights. Tubman's resilience in the face of danger and hardship shows that courage is born in the crucible of suffering. She was more than a survivor—she was a pioneer who changed the course of history.

Maya Angelou: From Adversity to Triumph

Maya Angelou's life was one of hardship and adversity. As a young girl, she was sexually abused and later became mute for five years as a result of trauma. She eventually regained her voice and went on to become one of the most influential writers and poets in American history.

Angelou's work - including her autobiographies and poetry - deals with themes of identity, trauma, and resilience. Her famous book, *I Know Why the Caged Bird Sings*, recounts her early life and struggles. Maya

Angelou's life is proof that no matter the depth of your wounds, healing and growth are possible. She became a beacon of hope for countless individuals, demonstrating that even the darkest of pasts does not have to dictate the future.

Aung San Suu Kyi: From Political Prisoner to National Leader

Aung San Suu Kyi's story is one of perseverance and sacrifice. A prominent political leader in Myanmar, she spent much of her adult life under house arrest for advocating for democratic reforms in the country. Despite being separated from her family and facing severe restrictions, Aung San Suu Kyi maintained her commitment to nonviolent resistance and became an international symbol for peace and democracy.

Her resilience eventually led to her release, and she went on to lead Myanmar's government as the country's state counselor. While her later political career has been controversial, her earlier struggle against military oppression reminds us that political activism rooted in peace and justice can bring about significant change.

J.K. Rowling: Depression to Best Selling Author

Before J.K. Rowling became one of the best-selling authors in the world, she struggled as a single mother, living on welfare and battling depression. During this period, she began to write the Harry Potter series, pouring her struggles and hopes into the story. When her manuscript was rejected by several publishers, she persisted, driven by a dream to create a life for herself and her daughter. When Harry Potter finally got published, it became an unprecedented success, transforming Rowling's life and bringing joy and inspiration to millions of readers worldwide. Her story embodies how passion and perseverance can lead to astonishing success, even when life seems bleak.

These ten women redefined what it means to overcome. Their stories demonstrate that even in the face of devastating hardship, a fierce commitment to personal growth and resilience can forge a path forward. By transforming their suffering into strength and purpose, they became powerful forces for change, each rewriting not only her own story but also inspiring millions to believe in their own capacity for resilience. In doing so, they have become living examples that adversity, while daunting, does not have to define one's destiny.

Chapter Twelve

Healing and Growth

Ultimately, the journey of a woman in the wilderness is one of healing and growth. Each challenge faced and every tear shed contributes to an evolving narrative that emphasizes resilience. As women embrace their vulnerability, they cultivate an emotional landscape rich with depth and authenticity. The story of Hagar serves as a powerful testament to the human spirit's capacity for rebirth, reminding mothers that they are not alone in their struggles. Through community, faith, and the reclamation of their narratives, they can navigate the wilderness of their lives, emerging stronger and more aligned with their true selves.

While every situation is unique and complex, there are certain proactive steps that can help women avoid, or better navigate, situations similar to Hagar's. Here are some practical strategies that can provide a sense of empowerment, stability, and protection for women, especially when it comes to family planning, relationships, and future security:

Know Your Worth and Set Boundaries

Understanding one's worth is foundational. Women should feel confident setting boundaries in relationships, particularly when it comes to respecting their own needs, dreams, and values. Recognizing and honoring one's worth can help to avoid situations where they may feel pressured into decisions that are not fully their own. Learning to assert one's boundaries around relationships, future planning, and intimacy can lead to healthier, more equitable relationships.

Pursue Education and Financial Independence

Financial independence provides a layer of security that can help prevent women from feeling trapped or powerless in challenging situations. Pursuing education, developing marketable skills, and establishing a career path enables women to have greater autonomy in making life decisions. Financial independence not only offers practical support but also builds confidence, which can strengthen women's ability to make choices that align with their values and long-term well-being.

Seek Healthy, Equitable Relationships

Choosing a partner who respects, supports, and shares similar values can help foster a mutually beneficial, loving relationship. Prioritizing qualities like empathy, honesty, communication, and respect in a partner creates a foundation of trust and mutual care, which helps avoid the dynamic of dependence or vulnerability that can leave one party at a disadvantage.

Consider Family Planning and Empowered Decision-Making

Taking control of family planning can empower women to make thoughtful decisions about parenthood. Educating oneself about reproductive health and discussing intentions with partners before serious commitments can help avoid situations where women feel pressured or unprepared. Access to family planning resources and the ability to make informed decisions are essential tools for any woman wanting to take charge of her future and the well-being of potential children.

Recognize Red Flags and Leave Early if Necessary

Cultivating an awareness of unhealthy relationship dynamics is critical. Red flags such as lack of respect, controlling behavior, manipulation, or dishonesty are